TOP 10 SPORTS BLOOPERS AND WHO MADE THEM

Jeff Savage

SPORTS TOP 10

Enslow Publishers, Inc.

40 Industrial Road   PO Box 38
Box 398   Aldershot
Berkeley Heights, NJ 07922   Hants GU12 6BP
USA   UK
http://www.enslow.com

Library of Congress Cataloging-in-Publication Data

Savage, Jeff, 1961–
    Top 10 sports bloopers and who made them / Jeff Savage.
        p. cm. — (Sports top 10)
    Includes bibliographical references (p. 46) and index.
    Summary: Presents profiles of ten athletes in various sports—including Bill
Buckner, Jose Canseco, Roberto de Vicenzo, Tonya Harding, Jim Marshall, Dan
O'Brien, Willie Shoemaker, Mike Tyson, Chris Webber and Garo Yepremian—
who each made a big mistake.
    ISBN 0-7660-1271-9
    1. Sports—United States Anecdotes Juvenile literature. 2. Athletes—United
States Anecdotes Juvenile literature. 3. Sports—United States Humor Juvenile
literature. 4. Athletes—United States Humor Juvenile literature. [1. Athletes
Miscellanea. 2. Sports Miscellanea.] I. Title. II. Title: Top ten sports bloopers
and who made them. III. Series.
GV707.S28   2000
796'.0973—dc21   99-34085
                                                     CIP

Printed in the United States of America

10 9 8 7 6 5 4 3 2 1

To Our Readers: All Internet addresses in this book were active and appropriate
when we went to press. Any comments or suggestions can be sent by e-mail to
Comments@enslow.com or to the address on the back cover.

Illustration Credits: Amateur Athletic Foundation, pp. 26, 29; © The United
States Golf Association, pp. 14, 17; Courtesy of the Boston Red Sox, pp. 7, 9;
Eileen Langsley, The Sporting Image, pp. 18, 21; Hollywood Park, pp. 30,
33; Jed Jacobsohn, Allsport, p. 35; John E. Biever, Minnesota Vikings, p. 25;
Miami Dolphins, pp. 42, 45. Michael Zagaris, Oakland A's, pp. 10, 13;
Minnesota Vikings, p. 22; The Sporting Image, p. 37; University of
Michigan, pp. 39, 41.

Cover Illustration: AP/Wide World Photos

Cover Description: Dan O'Brien

Interior Design: Richard Stalzer

CONTENTS

INTRODUCTION

NO ONE WANTS TO MAKE A BLOOPER. Sometimes a mistake happens anyway. As hard as athletes try, they can't win every time. They love to celebrate success, but they must endure failure, too. Because for every home run hit, there is a pitcher who surrendered it. For every touchdown scored, there is a player who missed a tackle. For every winning team, there is a losing one.

There are lots of books about the greatest plays ever made in sports. What about the worst plays? The worst mistakes? The worst bloopers? If you've ever played a sport, you know what it feels like to make a mistake. Everybody makes them. But what if the mistake you made was in front of thousands of fans or seen by millions on television?

Some bloopers are physical errors, like a dropped ball or a missed kick. Other bloopers are mental, which means they resulted from a poor decision or a momentary lapse in judgment.

Athletes hope to be remembered for their achievements. But no athlete wants to be remembered for a blooper. Unfortunately, the athletes who have committed the biggest bloopers, regardless of the great plays they made, will always be remembered for their mistakes. They will be reminded again and again for the rest of their lives of that precise moment when they goofed. Their blooper will forever be a source of pain, like touching a bruise. Football player Jim Marshall is a good example. Marshall was a star lineman who set several pro records, but he will always be remembered for running the wrong way with the ball to score for the other team. More than thirty years later, Marshall is still reminded weekly of his blooper. "People never talk about the other things I accomplished," he says.[1]

The most important thing about a blooper is how an

athlete responds to it. Some deny it was their fault. Others sulk about it. The athletes with true character are the ones who admit they blew it and go out and try harder. Jim Marshall is an example of that. One NFL (National Football League) official said: "His blooper is the story of someone who made a mistake, then bounced back to become one of the greatest players in NFL history. It's a blooper with a moral to it."[2]

A blooper is not an official statistic in sports. We don't keep track of bloopers like we do touchdowns or home runs. But when an athlete makes a blooper, we sure notice it. The bigger the blooper, the more we talk about it. We've compiled a list of the ten biggest bloopers we could think of. Perhaps you can think of others. We know these ten bloopers, and the athletes who made them, will be remembered forever.

ATHLETES AND BLOOPERS

NAME	SPORT	YEAR OF BLOOPER
BILL BUCKNER	Baseball	1986
JOSE CANSECO	Baseball	1993
ROBERTO DE VICENZO	Golf	1968
TONYA HARDING	Figure Skating	1994
JIM MARSHALL	Football	1964
DAN O'BRIEN	Track and Field	1992
WILLIE SHOEMAKER	Horse Racing	1957
MIKE TYSON	Boxing	1997
CHRIS WEBBER	Basketball	1993
GARO YEPREMIAN	Football	1973

BILL BUCKNER

THE BOSTON RED SOX NEEDED one more out. They were ready to celebrate their first baseball championship in sixty-eight years by winning the sixth game of the 1986 World Series. With two outs and nobody on base in the bottom of the 10th inning, and the Red Sox leading 5–3, even the New York Mets and their fans figured the game was over. The Shea Stadium scoreboard operator flashed "Congratulations Red Sox" on the big screen.

Then Gary Carter singled for the Mets. Pinch hitter Kevin Mitchell singled, too. Ray Knight was down to his last strike when he blooped another single to make the score 5–4. Bob Stanley uncorked a wild pitch to the next batter, Mookie Wilson, to allow the tying run to cross the plate. If that weren't enough for Red Sox fans to endure, next came one of the most horrendous errors in baseball history. Wilson tapped a roller directly at Boston first baseman Bill Buckner. At last the Sox would get the third out, right? Nope. The ball rolled right between Buckner's legs as if it were a croquet ball rolling through a wicket. The winning run crossed the plate for the Mets. The Red Sox lost Game 7 two days later and lost the Series.

Bill Buckner grew up in Napa, California, and began playing baseball almost before he learned to walk. He was so skilled by age seven that his mother, Marie, changed his birth certificate so he could join Little League a year early. "Pretty soon he was telling everyone what to do," said his brother, Bob. "Here was this little kid with freckles showing everyone how to do it."[1]

Buckner attended Napa High School, where he filled his

BILL BUCKNER

Bill Buckner still has not been forgiven by many
Boston Red Sox fans for allowing a ball to roll between
his legs in Game 6 of the 1986 World Series.

report card with A's and collected trophies for baseball and football. In 1968, his senior year, he was offered an athletic scholarship to the University of Southern California (USC). He was also drafted by the Los Angeles Dodgers. College or the minors? Buckner did both. He played in the Dodgers' minor-league system each summer and attended college in the fall. After joining the Dodgers' big-league club in 1971, he helped them to the 1974 pennant by batting .314. He hit to all fields and studied pitchers the way he studied books in school. As a result, he batted over .300 seven times in his career, including a National League high .324 in 1980. He was a relentless competitor, but sometimes he was too outspoken. After homering as a rookie off one pitcher, he said, "If they're all like this guy, I'll be all right."[2] The next time he faced that pitcher, he was decked by a fastball.

After committing that fateful blooper for the Red Sox, Buckner was hooted and booed everywhere he went. He played for the California Angels and Kansas City Royals before returning in 1990 for a final season with the Red Sox. He was given a standing ovation his first game back in Boston, but then the catcalls started again. Buckner felt he didn't deserve the harsh treatment. "Too many good things happened to me," he said. "Playing in the World Series. The All-Star Game. A batting title. A lot of good things." Even after he retired from baseball that year, the fans still would not let him forget. The harassment from people on the streets was constant, until, finally, in 1993, Buckner decided to move his family away from Boston. "Why put up with it? I'm tired of it," he said. "I don't want my kids hearing about it all the time."[3]

BILL BUCKNER

SPORT: Baseball.

BORN: December 14, 1949, Vallejo, California.

HIGH SCHOOL: Napa High School, Napa, California.

COLLEGE: USC; Arizona State.

PRO: Los Angeles Dodgers, 1971–1976; Chicago Cubs, 1977–1984; Boston Red Sox, 1984–1987, 1990; California Angels, 1987–1988; Kansas City Royals, 1988–1989.

ACHIEVEMENTS: National League batting title, 1980.

HONORS: Member of the Northern California Hall of Fame.

After his playing career was over, Buckner became a coach in the minor leagues.

Internet Address

http://fwp.simplenet.com/redsox/Players/bbuckner.html

JOSE CANSECO

With a mighty swing, Jose Canseco tries to put the ball in the seats.

FIELDING IS NOT JOSE CANSECO'S FAVORITE part of baseball. At the plate, he bashes home runs farther than almost anyone ever. On the base paths, he runs with confidence and often steals second or third base. But in the outfield, it's a whole different game. Canseco hopes to simply catch the ball and throw it back in without looking too goofy. Twice he has led the American League in errors by an outfielder.

No outfielder in the history of baseball ever looked sillier than Canseco in a game in 1993 while he was a member of the Texas Rangers. Canseco was in right field in Cleveland for a game against the Indians. Batter Carlos Martinez hit a high fly ball to deep right. Canseco drifted back to the warning track and settled under the ball. Right before he was about to catch it, he turned his head to look for the fence. He never should have taken his eyes off the ball. It came down and smacked him in the head and bounced over the fence for a home run. Canseco was not hurt. But he was very embarrassed. "Anybody got a Band-Aid?" he joked after the game. "I thought I had it...hit me in the head and bounced over. I'll be on ESPN ["Highlights"] for about a month."[1]

Jose Canseco was born in Havana, Cuba. He is an identical twin. Before he and twin brother Ozzie were a year old, his family fled Cuba for the United States. Canseco's favorite sports growing up in Miami, Florida, were soccer and basketball. He did not play baseball until he was thirteen. In high school he developed a solid batting stroke, but at five feet eleven inches and just 165 pounds, he was considered too skinny by most scouts to make the major leagues. But the Oakland A's took a chance and assigned him to their minor-league system.

Canseco began an intense weight-training program in which he packed about fifteen pounds of muscle a year onto his body. When he joined the A's as a major-league rookie in 1986, he was six feet three inches and 240 pounds. He gained fame with fellow slugger Mark McGwire, and together they were called the Bash Brothers because they bashed each other's forearms to celebrate home runs.

By 1988 Canseco was dominating the game. He became the first major-leaguer in history to hit 40 home runs and steal 40 bases in the same season. That year, he led the A's to their first of three straight World Series appearances. In Canseco's first World Series game he hit a grand slam against the Los Angeles Dodgers. But it was the only hit he got in 19 at bats, and the A's lost that series. Oakland swept the San Francisco Giants in 1989, but that World Series was tragically marked by a deadly earthquake. Canseco's team lost to the Reds in the 1990 World Series, and Canseco hasn't been back since.

That's not the sort of news Canseco wants to make. Nor does he want to be remembered for making a bonehead play in the outfield. But at least Jose can laugh at himself. "Hey, I'm an entertainer," he said after the ball bounced off his head for a homer.[2] Canseco laughed again when his teammate Jeff Huson said, "The [soccer] World Cup is coming to Dallas in 1994. Jose was just practicing."[3]

JOSE CANSECO

SPORT: Baseball.

BORN: July 2, 1964, Havana, Cuba.

HIGH SCHOOL: Coral Park High School, Miami, Florida.

PRO: Oakland A's, 1986–1992, 1997; Texas Rangers, 1992–1994; Boston Red Sox, 1995–1996; Toronto Blue Jays, 1998; Tampa Bay Devil Rays, 1999– .

RECORDS: First player in baseball to hit 40 or more home runs and steal 40 or more bases in the same season, 1988.

HONORS: Major League Rookie of the Year, 1986; American League Most Valuable Player, 1988; Comeback Player of the Year, 1994.

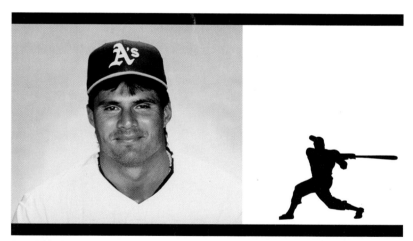

In 1988, Jose Canseco, then with the Oakland A's, became the first major-leaguer in history to steal 40 bases and hit 40 home runs in the same season.

Internet Address

http://www.devilrays.com/roster/2815.php3

ROBERTO DE VICENZO

Argentinian golfer Roberto de Vicenzo lost at the 1968 Masters tournament because he signed a scorecard that was incorrectly marked by his playing partner.

IT WAS ROBERTO DE VICENZO'S BIRTHDAY, and he was celebrating it with a brilliant round of golf. The forty-five-year-old pro from Argentina was delighting the fans at the 1968 Masters Tournament in Augusta, Georgia, with a string of superb shots.

De Vicenzo started the day in seventh place, but at the first hole he drilled a 9-iron into the cup for an eagle and was on his way. He made birdies at the second and third holes, and the gallery sang "Happy birthday, Roberto, happy birthday to you." He made four more birdies in the round, including shooting a 3 at the par-4 seventeenth hole. Millions watched on television as de Vicenzo tapped in a putt on the eighteenth hole to finish with a four-day total of 11-under-par, the fourth-best score in the history of the Masters. Minutes later, Bob Goalby finished with the same total score. To break the tie, tournament rules called for a full-round playoff the following day. But there would be no playoff.

One of golf's customs is for players to keep each other's scores. Playing partner Tommy Aaron kept de Vicenzo's score. Aaron accidentally wrote 4 instead of 3 as de Vicenzo's score on the seventeenth hole. De Vicenzo was so nervous and excited upon finishing his round that he hurriedly signed the scorecard that Aaron had kept for him without checking it. The total that he signed for was one stroke worse than Goalby's total. As de Vicenzo happily entered the press tent to talk with the media, a tournament official called him aside and told him the bad news. The rule is that if a player signs for a score on a hole that is better than actually played, he is disqualified. If a player signs for a score that is worse than actually played, the player must accept the worse score. De Vicenzo was stuck with a 4 instead of the 3 he actually shot. Goalby was given the victory. Aaron was terribly upset at marking down the wrong score, but de Vicenzo was a good-natured gentleman who blamed only himself. He did not speak perfect English, but everyone understood when he said, "What a stupid I am."[1]

Roberto de Vicenzo learned golf growing up in South America, where he began his successful pro career as the Argentine Open champion at age twenty-one. He later won the French Open, Belgian Open, Dutch Open, Mexican Open, Spanish Open, Brazilian Open, and even the prestigious British Open. A year after his British victory, he almost won the greatest tournament of all—the Masters. "I lose my brain," de Vicenzo said sadly about his blooper. "I play golf all over the world for thirty years. Never have I ever done such a thing before. Maybe I am too old to win."[2]

De Vicenzo was gracious about his blooper. Two years later, he received awards for distinguished sportsmanship in golf and significant contributions to the game. In a ballroom in New York, he was called to the podium amid applause and was handed a trophy. De Vicenzo studied the engraving on the trophy. Then he smiled and stepped to the microphone and announced, "Golf writers make three mistakes spelling my name on trophy. Maybe I not the only stupid."[3]

SPORT: Golf.

BORN: April 14, 1923, Buenos Aires, Argentina.

TURNED PRO: 1938.

JOINED PGA TOUR: 1947.

ACHIEVEMENTS: Seven-time Argentine Professional Champion, 1944–1945, 1947–1949, 1951–1952; six-time Argentine Open Champion, 1944, 1949, 1951–1952, 1958, 1967; British Open Champion, 1967.

HONORS: Bob Jones Award (for distinguished sportsmanship), 1970; William D. Richardson Award (for significant contribution), 1970; inducted into PGA Hall of Fame, 1979.

Though his famous blooper cost him the Masters, de Vicenzo had many other victories in his career, including the French Open, Belgian Open, Dutch Open, Mexican Open, Spanish Open, Brazilian Open, and British Open.

Internet Address

http://cnnsi.com/augusta/si_history_stories/1969-2.html

TONYA HARDING

In 1994, Tonya Harding was one of the United States' best women's figure skaters, before the scandal involving the attack on rival Nancy Kerrigan.

ON A SNOWY JANUARY AFTERNOON in 1994, the top American women skaters were gathered inside Cobo Arena in Detroit, Michigan, practicing for the U.S. National Championships. The top two finishers would win spots on Team USA for the upcoming Olympics. Tonya Harding was there. So was Nancy Kerrigan, Harding's chief rival.

Kerrigan had just finished a practice skate and had stepped off the ice when a shadowy figure approached from behind. Suddenly, without warning, he attacked. He swung a metal baton and struck Kerrigan violently in the leg. She crumpled to the ground, screaming "Why me? Why now? Help me! Help me!"[1] Stunned skaters and officials rushed to her aid. Kerrigan was taken to a hospital where she was diagnosed with deep bruises on her thigh and knee. In all the confusion, the mysterious attacker had escaped.

Who would do such a terrible thing? Police launched an investigation. Meanwhile, with Kerrigan unable to perform, Harding won the event and a spot on the Olympic team. Since Kerrigan was considered the country's best skater, and her leg would be healed in time for the Olympics, officials decided to award her the other spot. Soon chilling details of the assault began to emerge. The person who swung the club was a man named Shane Stant. The getaway driver was named Derrick Smith. Two other men, Jeff Gilooly and Shawn Eckardt, admitted to police that they had hired them to carry out the assault. Gilooly is Harding's ex-husband. Eckardt was her bodyguard. Gilooly and Eckardt claimed that Harding knew about the plan to injure her rival. At first, Harding denied knowing anything about it. A week later, she admitted knowing who the attackers were before they got caught yet chose not to report it to the police. She continued to deny that she knew about the plot to injure Kerrigan before it happened. People wondered if she was telling the whole truth.

Tonya Harding was born in Portland, Oregon, where she was raised by a father who was often unemployed, and a mother who was rumored to have been abusive. Harding's home address changed almost yearly. The only steady influence in her life was ice skating, which she began at age four. She was five foot one and 105 pounds when she stopped growing, and by then she had become an athletic whiz on skates. For instance, she was the first woman to perform a triple axel (a three-spin jump) in competition.

Controversy over Harding's involvement in the assault swirled. The clamor was embarrassing for the skating world. The U.S. Figure Skating Association considered barring Harding from the Olympics, but she threatened to sue, and officials backed down. The trouble did not end there.

At the Olympic Games in Norway, Harding broke a shoelace just before her performance. She was late getting on the ice and was nearly disqualified. In the middle of her routine, her lace came undone. She stopped her program and asked to be allowed to fix her skate and start over. The judges agreed. It did not matter. She skated poorly and finished out of medal contention. Meanwhile, Kerrigan performed beautifully and won the silver medal.

In the summer of 1994, Harding pleaded guilty to conspiracy to hinder prosecution of Gilooly and Eckhardt. She was sentenced to pay one hundred thousand dollars in fines and do five hundred hours of community service. She continued to deny that she helped plan the attack. Still, the U.S. Figure Skating Association banned her for life.

TONYA HARDING

SPORT: Figure skating.

BORN: November 12, 1970, Portland, Oregon.

TURNED PRO: 1986.

RECORDS: Fourth place at Olympic Games, 1992; first place at Skate America, 1991; first place at U.S. Figure Skating Championships, 1991, 1994 (title later stripped).

HONORS: Bill Hayward Award (Oregon's top amateur athlete), 1992.

Harding continues to deny that she was involved in the attack on Kerrigan. Nevertheless, she was banned for life from the U.S. Figure Skating Association.

Internet Address
http://espn.go.com/skating/index.html

JIM MARSHALL

Former Minnesota Vikings defensive lineman Jim Marshall was inspired to play even harder after he accidentally scored a safety for the San Francisco 49ers in 1964.

JIM MARSHALL

JIM MARSHALL WAS A FIERCE defensive lineman for the Minnesota Vikings who was so good at gobbling up fumbles that he still holds the record for the most recoveries ever. Unfortunately, it is what Marshall accidentally did with one of those fumble recoveries for which he is best remembered.

It was a blustery October afternoon in 1964 when the Vikings met the San Francisco 49ers at old Kezar Stadium in San Francisco, California. In the first half of a close game, the 49ers had possession at their own 35-yard line when they fumbled. Marshall saw the ball lying on the turf and beat half a dozen players to the spot. But in his haste to get to the ball, he had turned himself around. He scooped up the ball and took off running—toward his own goal! Radio announcer Lon Simmons screamed: "It's picked up by Jim Marshall who is running the wrong way! Marshall is running the wrong way! And he's running it into the end zone the wrong way. . . ."[1]

Thousands of 49ers fans were yelling, laughing, and celebrating. Marshall thought he had scored a touchdown. He thought they were cheering him on. He was so happy that he threw the ball into the stands to celebrate. Then his teammates reached the end zone and gave him the bad news. He did not score a touchdown. Instead, he had scored a safety for the 49ers. "I got turned around," Marshall said. "That happens in the heat of the game."[2]

Jim Marshall had learned to play football at an early age growing up in Columbus, Ohio. He starred at football and track in high school and college before moving north to join the Canadian Football League as a defensive lineman. A year later he was selected in the NFL draft in the fourth round by the Cleveland Browns, which kept him for just one season before trading him in 1961 to a newly created team—the Minnesota Vikings. Marshall joined Carl Eller, Alan Page, and Gary Larsen to form a ferocious defensive line that became known as "The Purple People Eaters." Over Marshall's entire pro career, which lasted two decades, he never missed a game.

One game Marshall probably wished he had missed was the one against the 49ers. But Marshall was such a smart player that he did not let his goof-up bother him. In fact, it inspired him to play even harder. In the second half of that game, he sacked 49ers quarterback George Mira so hard that Mira fumbled the ball, and Carl Eller ran it in for the game-winning touchdown.

After Marshall retired from pro football, he began working as a guidance counselor for children. One of the things he does is help troubled kids get back on the right track. He uses his wrong-way run as an example of how a negative can be turned into a positive. "One of the things I've tried to tell the young people I work with is that you can look at a mistake as an obstacle or an opportunity," Marshall says. "I took my mistake as an opportunity to prove I was a capable football player. When you make a mistake like that, believe me, you don't want to do it again. It helped me focus on being the best I could be."[3]

Thirty years after Marshall's blooper, football coaches, players, and sportswriters voted on the sport's biggest bloopers, and a video was made called "NFL's 100 Greatest Follies." Marshall's wrong-way run topped the list as the biggest football blooper ever. "It was a landslide," said Steve Sabol, the president of NFL Films, who counted the votes and produced the video.[4]

BORN: December 30, 1937, Danville, Kentucky.

HIGH SCHOOL: East High School, Columbus, Ohio.

COLLEGE: Ohio State University.

PRO: Saskatchewan Roughriders (CFL), 1959; Cleveland Browns, 1960; Minnesota Vikings, 1961–1979.

RECORDS: NFL career record for consecutive games played (282), most games played with one team (270), and most fumbles recovered (29).

HONORS: NCAA All-America, 1958; Pro Bowl selection, 1968–1969.

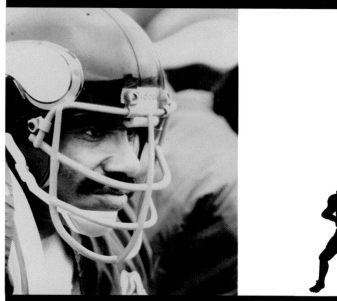

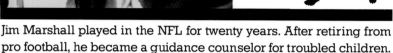

Jim Marshall played in the NFL for twenty years. After retiring from pro football, he became a guidance counselor for troubled children.

Internet Address

http://www.geocities.com/Colusseum/Arena/4677/vikings/history/vikings_profile_wrongway.html

DAN O'BRIEN

Dan O'Brien was expected to win the gold medal in the decathlon at the 1992 Olympics. He scored a zero in the pole vault during the Olympic Trials, however, and never made the team.

DAN O'BRIEN

THE 1992 OLYMPIC GAMES were still a month away, but Dan O'Brien was already a celebrity. O'Brien was half of the "Dan and Dave" advertising campaign by Reebok that featured the two top American decathletes in television commercials. O'Brien was the world champion and a good bet to win the Olympic gold medal. Dave Johnson was the Goodwill Games champion and likely to win the silver. Or maybe Johnson would win the gold and O'Brien would get the silver. Either way, a one-two finish seemed a cinch.

First, though, O'Brien and Johnson had to qualify at the U.S. Olympic Trials. The decathlon is a contest involving ten track-and-field events staged over a two day period. Competitors accumulate points based on their performance in each of the events. The top three finishers at the U.S. Trials would win spots on the Olympic team. As Reebok handed out thousands of "Dan and Dave" hats, T-shirts, and buttons to spectators in New Orleans, Louisiana, O'Brien and Johnson went about the routine of racking up points. Halfway through the meet, O'Brien had the lead and Johnson was second, leaving everyone else to battle for the third spot. Then O'Brien made an incredible blooper. He scored a zero in the pole vault.

Athletes score points in the pole vault by clearing the bar. The greatest height they clear determines the amount of points they get. They get three attempts at each height. At the U.S. Olympic Trials, the opening height for the pole vault was 14 feet, 5 1/2 inches. Athletes are permitted to skip early heights as long as they clear the first height at which they start. O'Brien figured the opening height was too easy for him, so he skipped it. The next height was 14 feet, 9 inches, and O'Brien passed there, too. He routinely vaulted nearly 17 feet, so he figured he would wait until the bar got higher. He skipped 15 feet, 1 inch, and passed again at 15 feet, 5 inches. When the bar reached 15 feet, 9 inches, O'Brien figured that was a good height to start. He sprinted down the runway with his pole, launched himself skyward toward the bar, and slammed into it. He missed! How could that be? *Fifteen feet, nine inches?* For O'Brien it should have been a snap. Incredibly, on his second attempt, he banged into the bar again. Suddenly he was down to his last chance. This time, he was so nervous that he went under the bar. O'Brien collapsed to the ground and cried. His Olympic dreams were shattered. "I felt real numb," he said. "It was devastating."[1]

Dan had lived his first two years in an orphanage before Jim and Virginia O'Brien adopted him and gave him their last name. Dan showed athletic skills very early. "The first thing he did after we got him was jump off a picnic table and start running," said Jim. Right then, Dan's mother predicted: "He's going to be in the Olympics."[2] Dan starred in football, basketball, and track during his school days, and he won a scholarship to the University of Idaho, where he struggled with college life for a time before dedicating himself to reaching the Olympics.

After his blooper in 1992, O'Brien grew more determined than ever to achieve his dream. Four years later, he cleared the bar in the pole vault and qualified for the 1996 Olympics. At the games in Atlanta, Georgia, when he completed the final event, the 1500 meter run, he collapsed to the ground and cried, just as he had four years earlier. This time they were tears of joy. O'Brien had won the gold medal.

DAN O'BRIEN

SPORT: Track and Field.

BORN: July 18, 1966, Portland, Oregon.

HIGH SCHOOL: Henley High School, Klamath Falls, Oregon.

COLLEGE: University of Idaho.

RECORDS: Broke American record with 8,812 points at the World Championships, Tokyo, Japan, 1991; broke world record with 8,891 points at DecaStar Meet in Talence, France, 1992.

HONORS: Decathlon World Champion, 1991, 1993, 1995; won silver medal at Goodwill Games, 1990; won gold medal at Goodwill Games, 1994; won gold medal at Olympic Games, 1996.

In 1996, O'Brien redeemed himself by winning the gold medal in the decathlon at the Olympic Games held in Atlanta, Georgia.

Internet Address

http://www.usatf.org/athletes/bios/obrien.shtml

WILLIE SHOEMAKER

Willie Shoemaker lost the 1957 Kentucky Derby by standing up in his stirrups and easing his horse, Gallant Man, before reaching the finish line.

WILLIE SHOEMAKER CLIMBED ABOARD his horse, Gallant Man, and rode it to the starting gate. This was the race Shoemaker was waiting for—the Kentucky Derby. Each year the best jockeys and horses gather at Churchill Downs in Lexington, Kentucky, to compete in horse racing's premier event. The 1957 race was loaded with fast horses, and "The Shoe," as he was known, thought he had the fastest. He was right.

Two years earlier, Shoemaker had won his first Derby aboard a horse named Swaps. A year later he became the first jockey ever to reach the $2 million mark in purse money. Shoemaker knew how to win. That's what made the outcome of this race all the more bizarre. Gallant Man came out almost last at the start. But Shoemaker knew what he was doing. He was saving Gallant Man's energy for a late burst. Shoemaker kept his horse close behind the pack down the backstretch. As the horses came around the last turn and started down the stretch, The Shoe made his move. Iron Liege was in the lead along the rail. Suddenly Gallant Man pulled even with Iron Liege, then moved past him. Gallant Man was going to win the Derby.

Then disaster struck. Shoemaker mistook the sixteenth pole for the finish line. He was still well short of the wire when he stood up in the stirrups and eased his horse back. He thought he had already won. Gallant Man slowed up. Iron Liege caught him at the wire. Photos revealed the awful news. Gallant Man had lost by a nose. Shoemaker was humiliated.

Willie Shoemaker was born in Texas, weighing just two

and a half pounds at birth, he barely survived. He began riding horses at age seven on his grandfather's ranch near Abilene, Texas. Later he moved to southern California. He weighed just eighty pounds in high school and failed to make the football and basketball teams. Determined to compete, he made the wrestling team and went undefeated. He also won a Golden Gloves boxing title. He left school after his sophomore year to work at a horse stable because his family needed the money. After a year of cleaning stalls and grooming horses, he realized that with his small size he could be a jockey. He entered his first race at age seventeen, and his career took off soon after.

Then came the blooper when Shoemaker stood up too soon in the saddle. "You can ask one hundred people and ninety of them can tell you who lost that Derby," he said, "but they can't tell you who won."[1] Shoemaker was suspended for fifteen days by Churchill Downs officials for "gross carelessness."[2] But just five weeks later, The Shoe rebounded to win another prestigious race, the Belmont Stakes, aboard Gallant Man. This time he made sure to stay seated in the saddle until the finish line. He went on to win more races and purse money than any jockey ever.

Fellow jockeys were impressed with the way Shoemaker handled his classic blooper. "He's the only one I know," said racing great Eddie Arcaro, "who could have suffered that kind of experience in a race like the Derby without going to pieces."[3] In fact, Shoemaker was so gracious after the episode that he was honored for his sportsmanship with the distinguished Ralph Lowe Trophy. Who was Ralph Lowe? He was the owner of Gallant Man.

WILLIE SHOEMAKER

SPORT: Horse Racing.

BORN: August 19, 1931, Fabens, Texas.

HIGH SCHOOL: El Monte High School, El Monte, California.

FIRST PRO RACE: Golden Gate Fields, Albany, California, 1949.

RECORDS: Won more races than any other jockey in history (8,833), 1949–1990; set career mark in all-time purse earnings ($123,375,524); led all jockeys in victories, 1953–1954, 1958–1959; led all jockeys in purse money, 1951, 1953–1954, 1958–1964.

HONORS: National Horse Racing Hall of Fame; president of the Jockeys' Guild.

Five weeks after losing the 1957 Derby, Shoemaker won the prestigious Belmont Stakes. He eventually retired as the winningest jockey of all time.

Internet Address
http://hall.racingmuseum.org/jockey.asp?ID=220

MIKE TYSON HAD BEEN KNOCKED OUT by Evander Holyfield in a boxing match eight months earlier, and now he was losing to Holyfield again. Tyson wasn't used to getting beaten. He was famous for landing big overhand rights and knocking opponents out. But after two rounds of the 1997 World Boxing Association heavyweight title fight in Las Vegas, Nevada, Tyson was being outboxed again by Holyfield. Tyson came out for the third round with a menacing glare. He was determined.

Tyson threw punches from every angle, but Holyfield blocked them all. It seemed there was no way Tyson could win. With a minute left in the third round, Tyson grabbed Holyfield in a clinch. Then Tyson spit out his mouthpiece. Nobody could believe what they were about to see. Tyson put his mouth up to Holyfield's right ear, opened wide, and chomped down on Holyfield's ear. He sank his teeth in and actually chewed off a piece. Then he spit it out. The 16,331 fight fans at the MGM Grand Arena and millions of viewers on television gasped in horror. Holyfield screamed in pain and hopped up and down. Tyson chased after Holyfield and shoved him from behind before referee Mills Lane stepped in. Lane sent the boxers to neutral corners and penalized Tyson two points. Then the referee let the bout continue. Within moments, Tyson grabbed Holyfield again and bit down on his left ear. A second chomp! The bell sounded right then, with Tyson standing in the middle of the ring and Holyfield staggering toward his corner with a pair of bleeding ears. The referee immediately stopped the fight, disqualifying Tyson.

MIKE TYSON

On June 28, 1997, Mike Tyson lost his composure and a chance at the heavyweight title when he was disqualified for biting off a part of opponent Evander Holyfield's ears.

Then Tyson went berserk. He screamed and punched wildly as police rushed into the ring. It took several minutes to restore order. As Tyson was led to his dressing room, he mumbled, "It's over. It's over. My life is over."[1] Meanwhile, Holyfield was taken to a hospital for surgery. A ring attendant had found the inch-long piece of his right ear that Tyson had chomped and spit out. Holyfield's ear was successfully reattached.

Mike Tyson was born in a ghetto in Brooklyn, New York, where he never knew his father. His mother despised violence and would not allow Mike to fight, and neighborhood bullies picked on him. "They used to take my sneakers, my clothes, my money," he said. "Beat me up and smack me around."[2] When Tyson was ten, an older boy tried to steal a pigeon he was raising, and Tyson beat up the boy. Tyson soon became a bully, and was sent away to a reform school, where he learned the basics of boxing. Legendary fight trainer Cus D'Amato took custody of Tyson at age thirteen and taught him the skills of the sport. Tyson turned pro at age nineteen and won a heavyweight title a year later. Over the next few years, he defeated all challengers but one, many with early-round knockouts. But he also experienced trouble outside the ring, starting with a marriage that lasted less than a year and ending with a violent episode that sent him to prison from 1992 to 1995. Tyson resumed boxing after his release, but his skills had eroded in prison.

Then came the horrific fight when the champ got chomped. A few days after that ugly bout, Tyson called Holyfield to apologize. The champion appeared to accept it, saying simply, "What happened is over and behind us."[3] But it wasn't over for Tyson, who was banned from boxing for more than a year and fined several million dollars.

MIKE TYSON

SPORT: Boxing.

BORN: June 30, 1966, Brooklyn, New York.

HIGH SCHOOL: Reform-schooled in Catskill, New York.

TURNED PRO: March 1985.

RECORDS: Became the youngest heavyweight champion in history, 1986.

HONORS: World Boxing Council heavyweight champion, 1986–1990, 1996–1997; World Boxing Association heavyweight champion, 1987–1990, 1996–1997; International Boxing Federation heavyweight champion, 1987–1990.

After the infamous fight with Holyfield, Tyson was suspended from boxing for one year and fined several million dollars.

Internet Address
http://www.MTyson.com

CHRIS WEBBER

CHRIS WEBBER WAS THE MOST FABULOUS PLAYER on the Fab Five. For the second straight year, he had led his young Michigan teammates to the college championship game. A year earlier, the five top-ranked freshmen, together called the Fab Five, reached the 1992 NCAA (National Collegiate Athletic Association) title game, only to lose to Grant Hill and Duke. This year the Fab Five was favored to win it. Webber was a big reason why.

Webber had led his team in scoring and rebounding all season. And with 23 points and 11 rebounds, he was doing it again in the title game at the New Orleans Superdome in Louisiana against North Carolina. But Webber's team needed to come through once more. Michigan trailed by two points with eleven seconds left. Webber had possession of the ball in front of his team's bench. The Wolverines could either tie or win the game. Then, Webber committed a horrifying blooper. He turned to the referee and signaled for a timeout. The problem was, the Wolverines had already used all their timeouts. They had none left. The players had been told so by their coach just moments earlier. Webber simply forgot. His lapse in concentration resulted in a technical foul. North Carolina was awarded two free throws *and* possession of the ball. The Tar Heels won, 77–71.

After the game Webber was seen sobbing in the arms of his family. He cost his team a chance to win the championship, and he admitted so later. "We had our hands on the trophy, but we had butterfingers," Webber said. "And I was the butter."[1]

Chris Webber was born in Detroit, Michigan, where

CHRIS WEBBER

In the 1993 NCAA Tournament championship game, Chris Webber called a timeout when his team had none left.

doctors predicted when he was still a baby that he would grow to be seven feet tall (he's six feet ten inches). When Webber touched a basketball for the first time at a summer-league program in sixth grade, he was teased mercilessly. "You've got the sorriest game I've ever seen," a boy named Jalen Rose told him.[2] Webber and Rose would later become Fab Five teammates. Webber worked hard to develop his game, and by eighth grade he had already received a dozen college recruiting letters. He led his high school team to the state championship as a senior and was voted National High School Player of the Year. After his sophomore year at Michigan he decided to turn pro and was the first player chosen in the 1993 National Basketball Association Draft. He has enjoyed a rich and successful pro career ever since.

But Webber's illustrious career will forever be marked by that one fateful timeout call. He remembers being so depressed over his blooper that when he returned to the Michigan campus, he could not go to class for three days. At a big family gathering at his grandmother's house a week later, Webber said he finally got over his misery after every-one went around all day making a "T" with their hands and saying "timeout" as a joke. "My family's never let me feel too sorry for myself," Webber said.[3] After joining the NBA (National Basketball Association), Webber showed he had forgiven himself and could laugh about his blooper. He formed a foundation for children called *Take Time Out*.

CHRIS WEBBER

SPORT: Basketball.

BORN: March 1, 1973, Detroit, Michigan.

HIGH SCHOOL: Detroit Country Day High School, Birmingham, Michigan.

COLLEGE: University of Michigan.

PRO: Golden State Warriors, 1993–1994; Washington Bullets, 1994–1998; Sacramento Kings, 1999– .

HONORS: National High School Player of the Year, 1991; NCAA All-America, 1993; first player chosen in NBA draft, 1993; NBA Rookie of the Year, 1994.

After the 1993 title game, Webber became the first player chosen in that year's NBA Draft. Webber won the Rookie of the Year Award in 1994 and made his first All-Star team in 1997.

Internet Address

http://www.nba.com/playerfile/chris_webber.html

GARO YEPREMIAN

During Super Bowl VII, Dolphins kicker Garo Yepremian tried to throw the ball during a botched field-goal attempt. The result was one of the most famous bloopers in Super Bowl history.

GARO YEPREMIAN

THE MIAMI DOLPHINS WERE NEARLY PERFECT. No NFL team had gone undefeated through a season, but the Dolphins were two minutes from winning Super Bowl VII and finishing with a perfect 17–0 record. The Dolphins led the Washington Redskins in the title game, by a 14–0 score, and were attempting to seal the victory with a field goal from the 42-yard line. The record Super Bowl crowd of 90,182 at steamy Los Angeles Memorial Coliseum could hardly believe what happened next.

Tiny Garo Yepremian lined up to attempt the kick. The ball was snapped, spotted, kicked . . . and blocked! It bounced right back to Yepremian. He tried to throw the ball, but it slipped from his hands and popped into the air. Then it came down and landed on his shoulder pads. "Many big people were chasing me," he said afterward. "I did not know what to do."[1] With the Redskins defenders bearing down on him, Yepremian panicked and batted the ball into the air. Washington's Mike Bass picked it out of midair and ran 49 yards with it for a touchdown. It was the craziest, zaniest, most hilarious play in Super Bowl history. But for Yepremian and the Dolphins it was a nightmare. Suddenly, Miami's chance for a perfect season was teetering. The Redskins got the ball again, but fortunately for Yepremian, Miami's defense kept them from scoring. The Dolphins won, 14–7, to gain their place in football history.

Garo's full name is Garabed Sarkis Yepremian. He was born in Larnaca, Cyprus, which is an island just south of Turkey in the Mediterranean Sea. As a boy, Yepremian attended a private school where he learned to speak English and play soccer. At age fifteen, he moved with his family to England, where he worked in a clothing factory, making neckties. At age twenty-two, he came to the United States to live with his brother, Krikor, in Frankton, Indiana.

Garo Yepremian and his brother heard that football teams were looking for kickers who could kick "soccer-style," or with the inside of their foot, rather than straight on with their toes. He wrote letters to several pro football teams asking for a tryout. The Detroit Lions signed him right away. Yepremian was little more than five and a half feet tall, kicked left-footed, and spoke little English. He said the reason he wore jersey number one was because it was the only numeral that would fit on his back. His Lions teammates thought he was funny, and they especially liked him the day he kicked six field goals against the Minnesota Vikings.

Yepremian joined the Miami Dolphins in 1970 and spent the next nine years making great kicks and setting team records. He ended the longest game in NFL history when he kicked a 37-yard field goal on Christmas Day 1971, to beat the Kansas City Chiefs, 27–24, in the *sixth* quarter, officially the second overtime.

Yepremian's Dolphins career ended after the 1978 season with many team records. After that he also played for the New Orleans Saints and Tampa Bay Buccaneers, but he is remembered most for his big blooper in the Super Bowl. As his teammates celebrated in the locker room after the game, Yepremian sat at his locker with his head down and muttered, "That championship ring will hang heavy on my hand."[2]

GARO YEPREMIAN

SPORT: Football.

BORN: June 2, 1944, Larnaca, Cyprus.

PRO: Detroit Lions, 1966–1967; Miami Dolphins, 1970–1978; New Orleans Saints, 1979; Tampa Bay Buccaneers, 1980–1981.

RECORDS: Lions record for most field goals in a game (6); Dolphins records for most career points (830), most field goals in a game (5), most consecutive field goals (16), and most consecutive extra points (110).

HONORS: Pro Bowl, 1971, 1973, 1978.

Despite his mistake in Super Bowl VII, Yepremian is remembered as one of the best place-kickers of the 1970s. He was selected to three All Pro teams from 1971–78.

Internet Address

http://dolphinsendzone.com/history/Dolphins72/gyepremian.asp

CHAPTER NOTES

Introduction
1. Vito Stellino, "Leon, Let Yourself Laugh About It," *Football Digest*, March 1994, p. 15.
2. Rachel Blount, "Biggest Blooper Ever?" *Minneapolis Star-Tribune*, December 23, 1994, p. 1.

Bill Buckner
1. Jim Kaplan, "He's Off in a Zone of His Own," *Sports Illustrated*, September 13, 1982, p. 51.
2. Ibid.
3. Leigh Montville, "The Scarlet Error," *Sports Illustrated*, July 26, 1993, p. 76.

Jose Canseco
1. Associated Press, "Going, Going, Boing, Gone," *The New York Times*, May 27, 1993, p. B13.
2. Ibid.
3. Tim Kurkjian, "Fool on the Hill," *Sports Illustrated*, June 7, 1993, p. 64.

Roberto de Vicenzo
1. Robert Sommers, *Golf Anecdotes* (New York: Oxford University Press, 1995), p. 246.
2. Alfred Wright, "I'd Be a Liar If I Said I Wasn't Happy," *Sports Illustrated*, April 22, 1968, p. 17.
3. Sommers, p. 246.

Tonya Harding
1. Louise Mooney Collins, *Newsmakers 94—The People Behind Today's Headlines* (Detroit, Mich.: Gale Research, 1994), p. 282.

Jim Marshall
1. Lon Simmons, San Francisco 49ers broadcast, KSFO-radio, October 6, 1964.
2. Vito Stellino, "Leon, Let Yourself Laugh About It," *Football Digest*, March 1994, p. 15.
3. Rachel Blount, "Biggest Blooper Ever?" *Minneapolis Star-Tribune*, December 23, 1994, p. 1.
4. Ibid., p. 3.

Dan O'Brien
1. Frank Litsky, "O'Brien Fails to Make Olympic Decathlon Team," *The New York Times*, June 28, 1992, sec. 8, p. 3.

2. William Plummer, "Ten-Speed American: Dan O'Brien Aims to Be the World's Greatest Athlete," *People Weekly*, August 19, 1991, p. 98.

Willie Shoemaker

1. Marc Pachter, *Champions of American Sport* (New York: Harry N. Abrams, Inc., 1981), p. 123.

2. Charles Moritz, ed., *Current Biography* (New York: The H. W. Wilson Company, 1966), p. 374.

3. Pachter, p. 123.

Mike Tyson

1. Mark Starr and Allison Samuels, "Ear Today, but Gone Tomorrow," *Newsweek*, July 14, 1997, p. 58.

2. Charles Moritz, ed., *Current Biography* (New York: The H. W. Wilson Company, 1988), p. 579.

3. Starr and Samuels, p. 58.

Chris Webber

1. Mike Lupica, "The Fab One," *Esquire*, November 1995, p. 50.

2. Louise Mooney Collins, *Newsmakers 94—The People Behind Today's Headlines* (Detroit, Mich.: Gale Research, 1994), p. 520.

3. Lupica, p. 52.

Garo Yepremian

1. George Solomon, "Nobody's Perfect," *Washington Post*, January 15, 1973, p. 8.

2. Tex Maule, "17–0–0," *Sports Illustrated*, January 22, 1973, p. 21.

INDEX